Irish Poems:
from Cromwell
to the Famine

Irish Poems:
from Cromwell
to the Famine

A Miscellany

Translated and Arranged by

Joan Keefe

Lewisburg
Bucknell University Press
London: Associated University Presses

© 1977 by Associated University Presses, Inc.

Associated University Presses, Inc.
Cranbury, New Jersey 08512

Associated University Presses
Magdalen House
136 - 148 Tooley Street
London SE1 2TT, England

Library of Congress Cataloging in Publication Data
Main entry under title:
Irish poems: from Cromwell to the Famine.
Includes Index.
1. Irish poetry—Translations into English.
2. English poetry—Translations from Irish. I. Keefe, Joan.
PB142.17   891.6'2'1008   76-755
ISBN 0-8387-1887-6

PRINTED IN THE UNITED STATES OF AMERICA

To the memory of my father

CHARLES TRODDEN

who introduced me to Irish literature

Some of these poems have appeared, in somewhat different form, in: *The Irish Press, The Kilkenny Magazine, The Journal of Irish Literature, Soundings '72* (An Anthology of New Irish Writing), *The New Orleans Review, The Faber Book of Irish Verse.*

Contents

Preface

From time to time in the past few years I have read or re-read Irish poems that strongly appealed to me and I was moved to re-cast them in English. The resulting miscellany is a personal selection, chosen according to my own response to the broad variety of work of a specific period. As such it should not be viewed as a comprehensive anthology of Irish poetry. My method of choice led, rather, to a group of poems that touch on a wide range of the feelings, concerns, and attitudes of the poets of the time.

Some translators are reluctant to depart from any construction in the original and, in the limit, tend to the crib or gloss form. Others take the original as a starting point for a "free" translation which sometimes involves significant license. Within the intervening spectrum, I have adopted no specific aiming point. Instead, for each individual poem I have tried to be guided, on the one hand, by a desire to stay as close in spirit to the original as possible, and, on the other, by a respect for English verse. The necessary compromise has been struck by my taste and depends upon the poem.

It is difficult to reproduce the original prosody of the Irish poetry, which is tuned to the ear and relies heavily on elaborate schemes of alliteration and assonance that give it its characteristic hypnotic quality of chant. Many of the poems were composed to fit traditional melodies and indeed are still known and sung. But they stand also as poems and it is as such I have chosen to treat them.

For the interested reader I include an original and a literal version of the first poem, "Forge me a Tool".

I would like to acknowledge the help of many friends while I was preparing this book. Professor Brendan O Hehir made welcome suggestions for which I thank him. I thank especially Professor Peter McConville and Professor Robert Tracy who read the manuscript and proposed several emendations. I am particularly grateful for the encouragement of Professor Thomas Flanagan. For his advice and unfailing patience, I thank my husband, Denis Keefe.

Introduction

The history of Irish poetry covers a period of well over a thousand years. The story of its growth, development, the assaults made on it by foreign infiltration and repressive laws, and its final fading in the eighteenth and early nineteenth centuries is, needless to say, a long and immensely complicated one. An account of those trends and events that had major influences on the lives and work of the poets included in this book must, of necessity, be brief and sketchy, but nonetheless may be helpful for a fuller understanding and appreciation of their poetry.

When Christian missionaries first reached Ireland they found an established pagan civilization with a fully developed system of laws, traditions and ceremonies, and a flourishing vernacular literature. The continuity of all of these structured elements depended on members of a highly respected professional class who can be described, with reasonable accuracy, as poets. There were degrees within the poetic class or order, each with its special duties and functions. They memorized and passed down to succeeding generations the laws, genealogies, the magic lore and charms, and the mythological histories and sagas. Once Christianity was well established by early medieval times, the monks enthusiastically began to record, in their vellums, much of this vernacular literature. In return, the native alliterative modes were enriched by traits adopted from Latin poetry. Rhyme appeared during this time and for the first time verse came to be used to express personal statement.

Toward the end of the twelfth century the Norman invasion of Ireland began the seven-hundred-year battle of language against language. For the first few centuries the native culture absorbed with ease the influx of Anglo-Norman and English influences. The Irish chiefs maintained their courts and their poets. But with the merciless depredations of the Elizabethans, the old order started to crumble. The few surviving Irish chiefs retired to the seclusion of remote country districts. Continuity was broken and society fragmented. In the next century Cromwell laid waste the country, and the Irish power was finally broken with the defeat of their armies, fighting for the Stuart cause, by William of Orange at the Battle of the Boyne in 1690. The native tradition held on stubbornly, but repressive laws against the language slowly took effect, and by the middle of the nineteenth century English was widely spoken and Irish was being forgotten.

Throughout these dreary centuries, some major factors contributed to the long resistance of the native literature to destruction. The ancient tradition of passing down by word of mouth the poems, sagas, myths, and stories, and the industrious habit introduced by the medieval monks of transcribing manuscripts, were two important elements. Another important and relatively late development (so far as is known) was the foundation of the "Bardic Schools" in the thirteenth century. These schools, where student poets composed in their celebrated windowless rooms, were the conservative guardians of traditional poetry. Innovation was frowned upon. Meter and form were strictly defined and had to be strictly adhered to. The most widely practiced form was an unrhythmically rhymed syllabic meter, but more ornamental meters were also used, which included stressed, alliterative, and assonantal elements. For three to four hundred years, these gallant schools husbanded and nurtured Irish poetry, albeit in a somewhat hothouse atmosphere.

The final break-up of the Gaelic order in the seventeenth century was accompanied by the disappearance of the Bardic Schools. Poetry became less the property of an elite and the literary need of the people came to find its main expression in the folk tradition of song. It is surmised that the Bardic poetry was chanted to harp music, though no trace of this kind of music remains. But, contemporary with the Bardic tradition, there existed a popular folk poetry set to harp melody, although it did not merit the attention of the professional poets. It was these hardier brands of song-meters allied to the remnants of the Bardic modes that became the poetic tool of the men who composed in this later period—the mid-seventeenth to the early nineteenth century—and who are represented here.

Our present original sources for most of these poems are tattered and fading manuscripts copied by scribes who contended with great difficulties as they pursued their dedicated labors. Sometimes they transcribed from other handwritten pages; sometimes they relied on their own memories or the memories of older people who recited the poems to them. They also had to face everyday hardship; one scribe gives an account of conditions in these affecting words: "The difficulty of working late, great haste, and a bad pen, as well as the darkness that is natural to night as distinguished from day, in which I wrote most of this, explain why it is not more elegant than it is."

We are fortunate that they continued their work for which they received ample thanks but little payment. They were the recorders of a despised and condemned culture. The ruling English and Anglo-Irish aristocracy had little time or use for the "native" language or literature. The poets themselves were spokesmen for a tradition that stretched back to pagan times but that could look to small hope of surviving into the future.

We know few certain facts about the lives of these Irish poets, but the meager details we do have allow us to surmise a biographical pattern. Their education was a haphazard business undertaken by devoted if unreliable poet-school-

[13]

masters at illegal hedge-schools. There, they learned, and learned to love, Irish history, poetry, traditions; they memorized genealogies and the ancient heroic and romantic sagas; acquired a smattering of Latin and Greek. Parents of sons who showed an aptitude for wit and learning were intensely proud of them. Often, money was scraped together and such sons were sent off to the great seminaries and monasteries of Spain and Italy to concentrate on religious studies. Just as often, however, the austere life was not much to their taste, and they returned home before ordination, to become schoolmasters in their turn. It was thus they could make a living, but their true vocation was poetry. They recited their poems to gatherings of friends, and to fellow-poets at "courts" of poetry, which met a few times a year. Many of their poems were memorized and passed into the folklore of the people to be remembered and sung long after the authors' names were forgotten.

Though the poet, working as schoolmaster, tutor, or even farm laborer, led a fragmented and sometimes painful life, he clung to a proud image of himself. A poet named Ó Rathaille (a kinsman of the great Aogán) gave this answer to an innocuous greeting:

"Sir, when you meet me at Mr. Power's, I am, it is true, but plain Mr. Rahilly, but I wish you to know when you meet me here, at Stradbally, on my own account, I am no longer Mr. Rahilly—but *Rake Outrageous O'Rahilly!*" (Quoted by Rev Patrick S. Dinneen in his introduction to *The Poems of Egan O'Rahilly* (London, 1911), p. xxxii.)

So they were rakes outrageous, living a life of wandering, drinking, and sporadic loving, but treated with admiration and an awe tinged with fear by the country people, because of their gift of poetry. (A long tradition from pagan times was the belief in the occult power of the word and in the magical powers of those who used the word. An ancient belief lingered that well-directed satire could raise blisters on a man.)

This rough biographical profile seems to fit such as Aogán Ó Rathaille, Eoghan Rua Ó Súilleabháin, Cathal Buí Mac Giolla Gunna, Seán Ó Coileáin, Aindrias Mac Craith, all of whom are represented in this book. There were exceptions, such as Seán Clárach Mac Domhnaill, who was a well-to-do-farmer and conducted "courts" of poetry at his home, gatherings that were anchorages for these drifting men. Piaras Mac Gearailt was another, a Fitzgerald whose family had once held extensive estates, and whose efforts to hold on to the remnant involved him in troublesome moral decisions. He convened his own court of poetry in his home district near Youghal.

At these schools or courts of poetry, the poets practiced and competed in the accepted forms and prosody. Meter and shape were still defined and the excellence of a poem was often judged on the poet's ability to include as much original wit and wordplay as the set form would allow. Within the boundaries of his tradition, the poet displayed his art and at the same time gave expression to his personal joy and suffering. In the hands of a master the music of the language is intricately enmeshed with the emotion, and the results are poems of the highest elegance and feeling.

The poets looked to tradition for form and sometimes for content, but for imagery they looked about them. A major feature of Irish poetry from earliest times that continued to shine through in this period is the intense, almost pagan involvement with nature—the contours of the hills and moors, the shape and promise of trees and hedges, the mood-changing aspects of wind, rain, sun, cloud. Where the emotion is clear and deeply felt, the images of nature are strong and organic, classical. In the three folk love poems included here, such is the case; the feelings are in the open, each poem has a view. Also, in the highly wrought and formal "Look to this Affair, Hugh," the images of nature weave a strength of realized emotion into the texture of the poem. In the "Lament for Oliver Grace" the symbols of fog, mist, darkness, and cloud all evoke loss and death in a way that permeates and informs the entire world of the poet. In a different mood and style the idea that nature confers freedom is voiced in a careless and happy manner in "What is it to Anyone?"

A strong and instinctive relationship with nature was not at all merely an artistic convention, but was shared and appreciated by uneducated country people. It might seem strange to a reader that the "Evicted Woman," as well as understandably mourning the loss of her household goods and treasures, should also bewail the loss of the cries of the wild birds, the sound of the streams, the aspects of nature that might appear to have a common ownership and not to be lost through eviction. But the words of the evicted woman were not histrionic. She understood well the future that lay ahead for herself and her family. The winter and hunger would soon drive them to the nearest town to beg for food and shelter. It was unlikely that they would survive long in the disease-ridden air where, in successive epidemics, fever killed hundreds of those weakened by starvation. The loss of the evicted woman is not exaggerated—she is indeed losing her whole world. The words she uses to express her sorrow are defined by the songs and poems that were part of her traditional lore. Her lament carries echoes of a poem written a century earlier by Seán Clárach MacDomhnaill:

> My cows are without shelter,
> My horses without grass or growth,
> My family lives in misery,
> Their elbows stick through their coats,
> The landlord is close at my heels,
> My shoes are full of holes,
> I have not a penny to mend them.

With their innate feeling for contour and texture, the poets watched with an angry sadness the changes wrought on the face of the countryside by the destruction of the forests. They wrote bitter poems about the fall of the trees and the effect it had on their own lives. Seán O'Dwyer is one such—his way of life has been destroyed along with

[16]

the woods. Sir Valentine Brown received 20,000 pounds for trees from his estate, but refused support for one who was the traditional family bard and one of the greatest of Irish poets, Aogán Ó Rathaille. The soul-destroying losses of his generation are summed up by Aogán in his famous poem "Valentine Brown."

The shape of the countryside included within it not only the earth itself, but houses, castles, and ruins, which sat easily on the land and became it. A strangely titled poem "Castle Cam" (literally "Twisted Castle") is called after a house perhaps, or a village. In a powerful poem of personal desolation Cathal Buí Mac Giolla Gunna uses it as a metaphor for the trammels of his life. Seán Ó Coileáin identifies his own old age and physical deterioration with the ruins of the Abbey of "Timoleague." Rather than give up the remnants of the confiscated Fitzgerald estates, Piaras Mac Gearailt changed his religion from Catholic to Protestant and wrote his "Answer to Thomas Barry," his apologia. His bewilderment at the thought that a just God might condemn Protestants for their beliefs is human and understandable. He clouds the main issue with a deliberately simplistic confusion of dogma, but the essential truth creeps in:

> I drew strife on my soul
> For love of earth.

In a people who loved land above God, the loss of land created hate, bitterness and cruelty—effects still part of the Irish scene. A moderate-seeming man like Seán Clárach MacDomhnaill was moved, at the death of a hated foreign landlord, Colonel James Dawson, to write a savage and relentless satire addressed to the stones on the man's grave.

Violent cause invokes violent response, but somewhat lesser evils (lesser only relatively) than a landlord like Dawson can be dealt with gracefully and expertly in poetic form. Eoghan Rua's need for a spade to enable him find work as a *spailpín* (itinerant laborer) evoked requests to his friend the blacksmith Séamus Mac Gearailt. The first, about the craft of the blacksmith, says much about the craft of the poet; the second is an ironic self-parody of the poet as con man of words. "Goodbye to the Maigue" by Aindrias Mac Craith, occasioned by his having to leave his home because of some vague wrongdoing, is a nostalgic and melancholy formal farewell.

The poets could laugh at themselves and one, Donncha Rua Mac Conmara, composed an entire comic world from the unpromising details of his harrowed life. His long poem, *The Adventures of a Miserable Wretch,* is a humorously mocking account of a disastrous trip abroad. From the first line, "I could tell famous stories to my friends," the scene is set for a lively caricature of the stereotype poet and his handling of the poetic conventions. Startling mixtures of half-baked learning abound. There are pointers to steer the reader in the right direction—the poet follows in the footsteps of "that brave old hero, Conán". Conán was the doltish strongman and muddleheaded clown of Fenian myth, subject to all kinds of personal humiliations. Contrasted with high-flown hyperbole are scenes of low comedy. There is a clever *Aisling* (vision) parody, in which the hero and the beautiful magic woman visit the underworld. There they meet a strange assortment of historical and mythological characters. Incongruously oblivious, Finn Mac Cool, Henry the Eighth, Romulus and Remus, Luther, Hercules, Ovid, and many others engage in a nightmarish repetitive pattern of characteristic action. Conán, playing the role of a loquacious Charon, conducts this tour and ends it with the conventional message of hope to the people of Ireland. With scarcely a pause for breath, the scene changes to a fierce sea-battle with French pirates. After buffeting, imprisonment, and loss of face, the hero is thankful to return to his native land.

One strange poem stands out from the rest because of its peculiar rhythmical and repetitive form. "The Midnight Flitting of Tomás MacGahan." It is a macabre song connected with Halloween and has a hypnotic ring to it that recalls mysterious ritual and druidic chants. Yeats has called this story "still the weirdest of Irish folk-tales."

The poems seem to fall naturally into an order covering the aspects of life in the Ireland they belong to. The language was dying and these poems reverberate with the disappearing cadences, melody, and movement of a poetic tradition that once had been a fitting tool for the imagination. A few decades after the latest of these poems was composed, the potato famines of the 1840s took their tragic toll. The nation was broken physically and spiritually. The promises of hope held out alike by the dashing soldier-scribes of the seventeenth century and the poor blind poet of Tipperary fell on ears deafened by hunger and fear. They could no longer hear or understand the clear voice of gladness.

Irish Poems:
from Cromwell
to the Famine

I
Countryside and Life

1
Forge me a Tool

From *Amhráin Eoghain Ruaidh Uí Súilleabháin* (The Poems of Eoghan Rua Ó Súilleabháin), ed. An tAthair Pádraig Ua Duinnín (Dublin, 1907), p. 53.

Eoghan Rua Ó Súilleabháin (1748–1784) was born near Killarney, Co. Kerry. He spent his life either schoolteaching or farm-laboring. About 1780 he may have spent some time in the English navy and army. He suffered a head wound in a fight in Killarney and this, complicated by fever, brought about his death in June of 1784. He was famous all over Munster as a poet and was one of the most inspired poets of the eighteenth century.

The poem is addressed to his friend the blacksmith, Séamus MacGearailt (Séamus Fitzgerald) requesting a spade, a necessary piece of equipment for the poet when he was going to the Hiring Fair to find work for the harvest season.

A Shéamais, Déan Dam

A Shéamais, déan dam féinidh arm na bhfód,
Sciuirse ghléasta dhéanfas grafadh 'gus romhar,

[25]

Stiuir ghlan éadtrom i bhfaobhar i dtathac 's i gcóir
Nach tútach gné is bhéas néata tarraingthe i gclódh.

I gclódh an airgid bíodh tarraingthe gan rian buille ar bith,
Scóip fada aici is leabhaireacht 'na hiarrachtaibh,
Sórd slaite bíodh leacuighthe ar a riaghail-chiumhasaibh,
'S is ró-thaithneamhach an t-arm liom faoi dhíormaibh.

A ciumhasa ma thígheann ná bíodh ortha scuilb ná ruic,
Is feicim a tígheal sleamhain slím i bhfuirm an tsuic,
Slighe an mhaide bíodh innti gan fuigheall ná uir-easbaidh
     ar bith
Is mar bharra ar gach nídh bíodh sí i mbinneas an chluig.

Literal Translation

O Séamus, make for me

O Séamus, make for me myself a weapon of the earth:
A ready instrument that will grub and dig,
A clear light guide in its edge, its strength and arrangement,
Not coarse in form and neat-shaped in appearance.

In the print of silver let it be shaped without the trace of
    any beat,
A long stretch in it and flexibility in its thrust,
A choice rod be embedded in its straight edges,
And very pleasant the weapon will be with me in the
    work-crew.

Its edges if it can happen let there not be on them cracks
    nor bumps,
And I see its smooth slim wing in the form of a point (beak),
The groove of the wood be in it without flaw or deficiency,
And as a top to everything, let it have the sweetness of a
    bell.

Forge me a Tool

Forge me a tool, my Séamus,
Fit for the earth,
A well-tempered spade
To work and till
Clean furrows, welded
To shape and hand-set.

No sign of beating mar
The press of silver steel,
Loose and free with flexible
Sweep, the grain
Of the wood-shaft tapered
To regular borders,
My tool will shine in the field.

No buckle or wrinkle
On the edges if possible,
I see its sleek flange
In the spare form of a beak,
The socket without flaw to take
The handle, the whole to have
Harmony like a bell.

Eoghan Rua Ó Súilleabháin

[27]

2
The Clear Voice of Gladness

From *Filíocht na nGael*, ed. Pádraig Ó Canainn (Dublin, 1958), p. 43.

Liam Dall Ó hIfearnáin (1720–1760) lived and died near Shronehill, County Tipperary. Although he never wandered far from his own village he was well-known to his fellow poets of Munster. His message of hope, in the poem given here, is a version of an *Aisling* (vision-poem). Generally the vision is described by the poets as being an apparition of a woman of surpassing beauty who fills the poet with hope and courage. Liam Dall was blind from an early age and his vision comes in the form of a voice of unearthly beauty. "John" and "George" are names of local foreign landlords.

The Clear Voice of Gladness

On the edge of the Great Wood
Under a thick cloak of grief
A voice drifted to my ears
With more wonder by far
Than harp music echoing,

Blackbirds' song in loneliness,
A more sweet music reached me
than ever was described,

Than the notes brought by scholars
Over the sea from Rome,
Than the chanting of wizards
In the hidden forts of spirits,
Than the early cry of cuckoos
From wooded hilly ledges,
All worry was removed from me
but that of small young Móirín.

A swarm of bees ransomed us,
Scrabbling for their sustenance,
So may their Autumn be sour
With no happiness for John,
George chased beyond the sea,
The crowd that was up-in-air
Without gold or property—
I will not pity their sad hour!

If I were buried in Shronehill
Firmly under a hard stone
And I heard this same message
So peacefully floating down,
With the force and strength of my shoulder
I would throw up the sods from me
And find my way back lightly,
Informed by that sound.

Liam Dall Ó hIfearnáin

3
What Is It to Anyone?

From *Dhá Chéad de Cheoltaibh Uladh* (Two Hundred Ulster Songs), ed. Enrí O Muirgheasa (Dublin, 1934), p. 239.

Author unknown.

What Is It to Anyone?

I went to the market and put my cow upon the block
For five pounds of silver and a yellow guinea's worth,
If I squander all the gold and fritter silver in the pub,
Oh, what is it to anyone whose business it is not?

If I walk to a wooded hill picking berries and brown nuts,
Shaking apples from the branches or herding sheep and
       goats,
If I stretch out to sleep for an hour beneath an oak,
What is it to anyone whose business it is not?

If I go to late-night parties for singing, games and sport,
To fairs and horse-races and gatherings of that sort,
If I see men drinking whiskey and I get tipsy too,
What is it to anyone whose business it is not?

Some are saying that I'm worthless, without success or
      future hope,
Without property or money, without store or dairy stock,
But if I take easy comfort, living in a hut,
What is it to anyone whose business it is not?

I have a lovely girl, patient, kind, and sweet,
Her throat is like the swan's, her cheeks are rosy red,
If she and I are under sail before the start of Lent,
Oh, what is it to anyone whose business it is not?

4
Friend of my Heart

From *Amhráin Eoghain Ruaidh Uí Súilleabháin* (The Poems of Eoghan Rua Ó Súilleabháin), ed. An tAthair Pádraig Ua Duinnín (Dublin, 1907), p. 54.

Another request for a spade, to his friend the blacksmith.

Friend of my Heart

Friend of my heart, Seamus, loving and witty,
Of Geraldine blood, Greek-tinged and poetic,
Make me a clean smooth handle to fit my spade
And add a nice crook as a crowning elegance.

Then I'll shoulder my tool and go on my way
Since my thirst for adventure has not been quenched
Without stop with my spade as far off as Galway
Where daily my pay will be breakfast and sixpence.

Before the day's end if my tired bones give out
And the steward says my grip of the spade is in doubt,
Then calmly I will tell him of the adventure of death
And of classical battles that left heroes weak.

[32]

Of Samson and high deeds I will talk for a while,
Of strong Alexander eager for enemies,
Of the Caesars' dictatorship, powerful and wise,
Or of Achilles who left many dead in the field,
Of the fall of the Fenians with terrible slaughter,
And the heartbreaking story of ravishing Deirdre.
And then with sweet coaxing I will sing songs,
An account of my day you have there now, Seamus.

After my labor I'll take my pay in a lump
And tie it with hemp in the breast of my shirt,
Still with a high heart I will head straight for home,
Not parting with sixpence till I come to your forge.

You are a man like me tormented with thirst,
So we will briskly set off for the inn down the road,
Ale and drams I will order to be arrayed on the table
And no ha'penny of hard-earned money will be spared.

Eoghan Rua Ó Súilleabháin

5
Sean O'Dwyer of the Glen

From *Irish Minstrelsy,* by James Hardiman (Dublin, 1831), 2:86.

The O'Dwyers held land in the barony of Kilnamanagh, Co. Tipperary and fought a losing battle against the Cromwellian armies in 1650–1652. It is likely that the Sean O'Dwyer of the song shared a fate similar to that of his cousin Colonel Edmund O'Dwyer who, after the defeat of the Irish cause, left Ireland to fight and die in the service of foreign armies. The words of the song tell us that Sean O'Dwyer of the Glen, as he witnesses the steady destruction of the forests, foresees that he too will soon be forced to leave.

The Glen referred to is probably the Glen of Aherlow, which was settled by Cromwellian adventurers, among them the Dawson family, about whom another poem was written (no. 19).

Sean O'Dwyer of the Glen

Rising in the morning
The summer sun shining,

I have heard the chant weaving
And the sweet songs of birds,
Badgers and small creatures,
The woodcock with his long beak,
The sounding of echoes,
The firing of strong guns,
The red fox on the crag,
Thousand yells of huntsmen
And a woman glumly in the pathway
Counting her flock of geese,
But now the woods are being cut
We will cross over the sea
And, Sean O'Dwyer of the Glen,
You are left weak.

This is my long loneliness,
The shelter for my head being cut,
The North wind lashing me
And death in the sky;
My happy dog being tied up
With no right to move or gambol
Who would take bad temper from a child
In the bright noon day;
The hearts of nobles on the rock
Capering, proud, prancing,
Who would climb up beyond the furze
Until their final day.
So if I get a little peace soon
From the gentry of the town
I will make my way to Galway
And leave the rout behind.

Meadows in stream-cut valleys
Have no vigor, no strength of men,
No glass or cup is raised
To health or happy life;
My bare hills! loss of hedges

[35]

From low field to mountain stacks
Leaves the hare on thickets' edges,
A vagrant on the plain.
What is this raid of strangers
But long-drawn cutting and clearing ?
Sweet-whistled thrush and blackbird
Without branches for their singing,
An omen of coming troubles
Burdened priest and people
Adrift in empty harbors
Of deep mountain glens.

This is my daily bitterness,
To have lived to the age of sin,
To see this heavy scandal fall
On my people, my own kind.
How often on those long fine days
There were apples on the trees,
Green leaves on the oak,
Fresh dew on the grass;
Now I am driven from my acres,
In lonely cold without friends,
Hiding sadly in holes
And hollows of the mountain.
If I don't get some peace soon
And the right to stay at home
I must give up my own ground,
My country and my life.

6
Small Beer

From *Filídhe na Máighe* (The Maigue Poets), ed. An tAthair
Pádraig Ua Duinnín (Dublin, 1909), p. 38.

The Maigue is a river in Limerick and gives its name
to the surrounding countryside. In the eighteenth century
it was a center for poetry and poets. Its two most famous
poets are Seán Ó Tuama (1706–1775?) and Aindrias Mac
Craith, his contemporary, friend, and poetical sparring
partner. They engaged in versified disputes that often, though
starting agreeably, ended acrimoniously. In this case, Ó
Tuama had written a poem complaining about the trials of
his life—he was an innkeeper as well as poet—his customers
would not pay, they distracted him with their songs, they
were disorderly and rowdy. Mac Craith replied to this with
an attack on Ó Tuama, "sly John," in his role of both poet
and host. Part of this reply is translated here as "Small Beer."
Further and more bitter poems shot back and forth—Mac
Craith being finally beaten into English bombast:

"If you are so reduced as not to shew a farthing in
your poetical purse, turn broker and get your living as
auctioneer, sell the lumber set out to public sale to those
about you, such as old shoes, bristles, stinking fish and

[37]

the like, or, if you choose, turn rag-gatherer, porter, or common scullion, and clear the streets of rubbish."

Small Beer

You are a man who trades in small beer
Without body or substance, and brandy
That gives your customers nightmares
With memories scattered in frenzy.

Bad ale you purvey every day as good porter
That your wife decants in scant quarts,
Your jokes drive the company crazy with boredom
So they take off on meandering walks.

When yourself, you pour your scarce pints
The glasses are half filled with froth
So soon we're not able to sit at the table
Nor take the road home without props.

And, as well, it is true you delude
Your companions with slippery talk,
You drive us all mad with your foolishness,
Your unceasing gabble and chat.

The old bards are my heartbeat and pulse,
Not the rickety lies of sly John,
A tyrant in taste and confused on facts
Your verses are half-true or wrong.

Your poems and rhymes have no class
And your meters are clumsy,
With too many measures unfilled in your glasses
And ditch-water lacing your brandy.

Aindrias Mac Craith

[38]

II

Love – Lost, Divided, Mourned

7
No Sleep my Sleep

From *Dhá Chéad de Cheoltaibh Uladh* (Two Hundred Ulster Songs), ed. Enrí Ó Muirgheasa (Dublin, 1934), p. 97.

Author unknown.

No Sleep my Sleep

No sleep my sleep,
no rest my fitful rest,
no sleep I slept
through last night's hours,
with waves of pain
sweeping through my breast;
could anyone suffer this
and not be crazed?

Blackbird, you keep your heart
easily in one piece,
lightly you sleep
both night and day;
I am not thus,

[41]

such pains torment me,
my heart consumed
in the harshness of my fate.

My Love, do not desire
to gain a stately lady,
though airily she dresses
her grace is quickly gone—
so blithely steps the peacock
yet no one picks his bones—
many women are false toys,
of benefit to none.

My Love, if you will come
and steal away with me
I will give you brown sugar
and honey of the bee,
if this island were all mine
I would give it to you whole,
long life will not be mine, heart's love,
if you leave me alone.

8
A Long Way from the House

From *Dhá Chéad de Cheoltaibh Uladh* (Two Hundred Ulster Songs), ed. Enrí Ó Muirgheasa (Dublin, 1934), p. 98.

Author unknown.

A Long Way from the House

A long way from the house
I would know you by your walk
And the set of your hat
On your head,
Once your kisses were honey
In the morning, mourning you
Will soon cause my death.

I go out to the back of
The house every day
To search for a trace
Of you coming
While they're digging for me
A long narrow grave

Where the green grass and nettles
Through my heart will be growing.

O, my love with eyes greener
Than fresh growing reeds
My grieving would not cease
If I heard of your fate,
Gather together on one hill
All the young men of Ireland
Your hand is the one I would take.

9
If I Left for the West

From *Love Songs of Connaught* by Douglas Hyde (Dublin, 1905), p. 4.

Author unknown.

If I Left for the West

If I left for the West
I would not come back,
Climbing the highest hill
The freshest branch first
I would gather and make
My way quickly
To him I love most.

My heart is dark
As a sloe or as coal
For the forge, or the soles
Of my shoes leaving marks
On white halls,
And sad notes
Sound in my laugh.

[45]

My heart is frittered
Like ice shattered
On the water's surface,
Like hazel nuts littered
And scattered,
Because of disgrace
A girl's heart embittered.

Sweet blackberries bring
The taste of my love
And raspberries red
In the sun, shining
Bilberries growing on the hill,
Many times a dark head
Lay on fair skin.

It is time that I leave
This place where the stones
Cut sharply and the mud
Is cold and I hear
Voices closed
To kindness, and the word
Of backbiting and calumny.

Love I denounce, and regret
That woman's son
Had mine and renounced
It and left
My heart sunk
In sorrow, and down
Or up the road I am bereft.

10
Stars are Standing

From *Duanaire Gaedhilge* (An Irish Anthology), ed. Róis ní Ogáin (Dublin, 1921), p. 39.

Author unknown.

Stars are Standing

Stars are standing about the sky
Together the sun and moon are lying low
Ebbing tide deserts the inlets where
The swan no longer holds his course,
The cuckoo in tangled branches
Monotonously cries "She's gone,"
My love with the long smooth hair
You leave the country forlorn.

Three things, I see, that come from love
Are sin and pain and death,
My instinct daily tells me
You misted my mind with hurt,
Dear love, you tilted my reason but

My hand can turn a prayer
To mend the flint wounds in my heart
May God give you the grace.

11
Leave Aside your Weapons

From *Dánta Grádha,* an Anthology of Irish Love Poetry
(A.D. 1350–1750), collected and edited by Thomas F.
O'Rahilly, (Cork and Dublin, 1926), p. 34.

Piaras Feiriteir (1610–1653) was a soldier-poet in the courtly
tradition. He lived at the time the strict syllabic meters were
giving way to the looser, heavily stressed song meters, and
he composed with distinction in both modes. He was hanged
in Killarney for rebellious activities.

Leave Aside your Weapons

Leave aside your weapons, lady,
Unless you wish to ruin all,
Unless you put your weapons by
I must bind you fast for safety.

If you would put your weapons by,
Then hide your curling hair,
Your white throat do not leave bare,
Let no one glimpse them lightly.

If, brave lady, you surmise
You kill none north or south,
A tear from your bright eyes
Kills all, no need for sword.

Truly the smooth sheen of your knee,
And even more your tender palm,
Each one seeing them is harmed,
Shield and spear could not do more.

Your lime-white breast conceal from me,
Your gleaming sides do not uncover,
For love of Christ let no one see
Your breasts so bright as bramble flower.

Hide from me your eyes like arrows,
Lest I die for you through them,
For sake of soul seal tight your lips
So your bright teeth may not be seen.

If enough you've rendered weak,
Before the grave enfolds us,
Lady, conquering all before you,
Leave now these weapons from you.

Piaras Feiriteir

12
Look to this Affair, Hugh

From *Dánta Grádha,* an Anthology of Irish Love Poetry
A.D. 1350–1750, collected and edited by Thomas F. O'Rahilly
(Cork and Dublin, 1926), p. 55.

The manuscript of this poem exists in tattered form,
dated 1674, but the poem itself may be much older. There
is controversy as to its real meaning and purpose. Some
scholars believe that it is, in fact, not at all the apparent
cry of a woman torn between husband and lover, but an
example of the poetic conceit whereby the poet addresses
his patron.

Look to this Affair, Hugh

(The poem is addressed to her husband Hugh O'Rourke,
son of Brian, and to her lover Tomás Costello, son of
Siúrtán.)

I

Look to this affair, Hugh,
Flower of the fairest bough,

[51]

Brave shoot of strongest root,
Look to what Tomás is at.

Hurry Hugh, look after me
If you are faithful,
Here is the magic knight
Tempting me in whispers.

Mac Brian, believe my words
If you would not lose me,
Help me then, beloved rib,
Reprimand the son of Siúrtán.

Tell him, make him comprehend
No poet's need I pursued,
As a virgin wife from Cara
I am possessed by only you.

Now that he is after me,
This honey-worded tempter,
No matter what he promises
Do not think he will not lure me.

Your opinion, not mine,
That this poet-thief of Ireland,
A lion mauling my thin will
Is not wrenching my compliance.

If affection seduce me,
Then, Hugh, understand
By the Hound of Conn
I cannot abandon him.

Often magic of enticement,
His pleasure unmistakable,
Hidden in a poet's pose,
Toward me is directed.

[52]

Often, then, he comes to me,
Swooping like a hawk
Through a crowd to grab my heart,
A sorcerer, to me a saint.

As if I were a tinker girl
That he would pleasure,
With magic words and evil rhymes
He pleads with me to go with him.

He comes as a man,
He comes as a spirit,
He comes as a soul,
What way can I avoid him?

While abroad, on my behalf,
Men fight for victory with O'Neill,
He wins my love by trickery
Feigning love for other women.

Then in your form, Hugh O'Rourke,
He comes free in every move,
A gentle dragon trailing bonds,
Deceiving me with love.

But with Tomás himself
Without disguise, I lose my sense,
So dear is he to me
My heart is wrested from its place.

    Unless you understand
    And help me
    Dearest love
    I am won over,
    No way can I divide
    Myself between you;

[53]

Hugh, my soul is in your cage,
Tomás, my body is enchained.

II

No good my repeating
"Go, dear Tomás,
Though loving others, do not betray
Hugh's friendship for my sake,"

Or saying "My proud Tomás,
Pledge of Costello's faith,
Leave me, I am true,
Love others, I love Hugh."

I am no easy woman
You can coax in your arrogance,
Your bright heat cannot melt me,
Though hot as summer sunlight.

Do not believe I am a whore,
My husband had me first
And since then only Hugh,
Send me no meaning looks.

Your wild lust will not prevail,
I know your many shapes,
Thief, do not destroy me,
Turn, plunderer of smiles.

No ease from me,
Little thief, little liar,
Your strength has no dazzle,
Find a victim elsewhere.

[54]

And know, son of Siúrtán,
Fragrant plant of the wood,
No love, no pride, no gold
Can shift me from Hugh.

Since we cannot be together
Pursue your native craft,
Increase the heroes in your image,
Heroic lover you will remain

. . . .

My leader useful in war
My generous giver of joy
My pool of all plenty
My master of swordplay
My steady mast of war-sails

Clever maker of heartbreak
Spring of sure death
Fierce battering wave
Tongs of love's embers
Murmuring mover of woman—

If I am yours could I admit it?

Tomás, my defense has come to this:
Strong Costello,
My heart is saying
To drink of love
If I would drink.

My wishes with you and all my will,
Fair-haired lover do not betray
Or damn my peace with jealousy.

We must part
Weary sorrow

Hugh comes to see me
Pass by quickly
Pity the need
Alas

Do not look.

13
Lament for Oliver Grace

From *Irish Minstrelsy*, by James Hardiman (Dublin, 1831), 2:245.

Laments on the death of a patron or a member of his family were composed by the poets in a formal elegiac style. Certain phrases and expressions of grief became fixed and were repeated over and over. Hardiman thinks that this poem was composed by a kinsman (Seán Mac Bháitear Breathnach) on the death of Oliver Grace in 1604. But it is probable that the poem is of much later origin and it may be an amalgamation of different laments. One inconsistency in the version given by Hardiman is that the sound of waves is mentioned, but Kilkenny, where the Graces lived, is many miles from the sea. Whatever its true history, the poem seems to be a real expression of grief for the loss of a young man.

Lament for Oliver Grace

A black fog on the mountain
Never seen there before,

[57]

Heavy silence at noon
Broken by the drone of grief,
A bell of death on the wind
O God! the messenger of sorrow,
Cawing of the black crow
Tells the passing of the dead.

Was it you, my young lord, my love,
The banshee wailed so sadly
In the lonely quiet of the night—
Was it you she was keening?
The cliffs and the salt waves
Echoed back to us her crying
And no cock crowed at dawn
To tell us time or tide.

O, young Oliver, my darling,
It is your death she keened,
Your death turns day to night,
Your death begins our grief.

And this is why I weep,
That our hope turns to despair,
Always tears now, tears pouring down,
Our future holds our heartbreak.
Death, you have withered
The flower of our highest branch,
Alas, you earned your dismal pay,
He goes alone into the grave.

It should not be the fate of a young man
To go into the grave alone,
To draw out her day with grief
And life with heartbreak for his wife.
She will bear and foster sorrow
By her children's father, her first lover
Leaving her heavy with no child but death,
To lie too soon on a cold clay bed.

[58]

He will not again follow the deer
Through shadowy glens and up hills of mist,
His horn will not be heard rousing sound
Nor the noise of the hunt from the mountain,
He will not be seen on his galloping horse
Cutting a path over ditch and hedge,
His way is now changed for ever,
The heavy fog has closed on his spirit.

This impenetrable fog of sorrow
Is a shroud that covers Courtown
And stills the heart of a kindly lord
Pierced by the death of his firstborn son,
Who was his heir in glory, name and power,
Like a strong young oak tree with promise
Of widespread and protective branches.

His generous hand lies languidly,
His intelligent heart is powerless
Who was the son of heroes, the friend of poets,
The beloved of musicians.

> Your fame needs no glow of song
> But words enlighten my grief,
> At the end of the elegy we weep.
> On the tomb of our beloved
> My heart breaks.

Seán MacBháitear Breathnach(?)

III
Rejection and Reflection

14
An Answer to Thomas Barry

From *Amhráin Phiarais Mhic Gearailt,* ed. Riseárd Ó
Foghludha (Dublin, 1905), pp. 46–47.

An accomplished poet in Irish, Piaras MacGearailt
(Pierce Fitzgerald) (1709–1791) was leader or "High-Sheriff"
of a famous Court of Poetry that was convened a few times
a year in his home district near Youghal. The Fitzgeralds
had once owned large estates but most had been confiscated
by the time Piaras inherited. To save the last remnants he
chose to give up his Catholic religion and turn Protestant.
This provoked an attack in verse by one Thomas Barry, a
poet of Clonmel. " To Thomas Barry" is Piaras MacGearailt's
reply.

An Answer to Thomas Barry

Dearest Barry,
My clever friend,
Going over to Calvin
Is my cross to carry
Because my children's loss

[63]

Of acres and herds
Left my life a stormy
Heartstream of tears.

Too long has this wrong
Lain on our chiefs,
They are rent, impoverished
And crushed into weakness.
Bright God, if you don't trample
On these foreign boors
Soon all our landowners
Will follow my sad move.

This is a sickness and hurt
Wounding me, never
Ceasing cutting to
My lungs and my liver,
That rather than my children
Be sunk in the dirt
I drew strife on my soul
For love of earth.

Do not harbor anger
In your minds for me,
Enough that Heaven's wrath
Is launched, my friends,
And to guard my soul
I urge the Son of God;
Though I am a sinner
Sunk in the world's mire,
Fettered in the world's chains,
Still to the mild nurse
Of Christ I cry
"Dispel my sighs,
Relieve me of this curse!"

My faith has done me harm
In a way that is not fitting,

And to avoid it for land
Cannot be a proper thing,
I claim it is unfair
And pray now without fail
For help from the unchanging King.

O dear friend, remember
I was a creature cornered,
Though to your mind
Merely a man deluded,
But fines and rent and tax
And costs of litigation
Made many more than me
Cross the road to Luther.

Piaras Mac Gearailt

15
Castle Cam

From *Dhá Chéad de Cheoltaibh Uladh,* ed. Enrí Ó
Muirgheasa (Dublin, 1934), p. 245.

Cathal Buí MacGiolla Gunna (1666–1756?) was a Cavan
poet and "a wild rover that stopped at nothing." During his
disreputable life he had many escapades with women, some
unhappy, as seems to be the case in this poem. He wrote
one of the finest poems in Irish "An Bonnán Buí" (The
Yellow Bittern). It is said that he wrote his last poem
when he was on his deathbed. With neither pencil nor paper,
nor any one to help him, he reached for a charred stick
from the fireplace and wrote his last lines on the wall beside
his bed.

Castle Cam

A heavy load of dreams
Rests on my sleeping wife,
She is lost to me drowning
In her high-pitched nightmare,
There is no chance now of repentance

For the lies I've told—
Listen to the wind grow strong,
If people only did their share
They would prop the creaking wall—
Little I thought this time last night
They would let me die in Castle Cam.

I am not wise and paid the rent
Before the time was due,
If I could get it back no penny
I would spend, but at the bottom
Of the hedge I'd find a refuge.
Give me my share before
My hour arrives and then divide
The rags between the wife and child,
Little I thought this time last night
They would end my life in Castle Cam.

If fire should strike me waking
I would roar like a baited bull
But if it should creep behind me
While I slept, then Castle Cam
Would wait and watch me burn,
I would rather have a sword
Pierce my ribs and lay me stretched
On the floor with no thought left
Than to be alone in the midst of them
Trembling in the night in Castle Cam.

Cathal Buí Mac Giolla Gunna

16
Timoleague

From *Measgra Dánta* (Miscellaneous Irish Poems) 2, ed. Thomas F. O'Rahilly (Dublin and Cork, 1927), p. 158.

Little is known with certainty of the life of Seán Ó Coileáin (1754–1816). He studied for the priesthood but instead of becoming a priest he married and opened a school in Myross in West Cork. He seems to have led a wasted and sad life. He is buried at Kilmeen where he was born, not far from the ruins of Timoleague Abbey.

The Franciscan Abbey of Timoleague was founded in 1312 and lasted with some interruption until its final burning by the English in 1642. It was a center of trade as well as learning. Smith in his *History of Cork* describes it as having been "formerly a place of some note, being much resorted to by Spaniards, who imported large quantities of wine here." After the extinction of the Abbey, the town around it declined to little more than a village. The ruin is one of the most impressive and beautiful landmarks in Ireland.

Timoleague

One night I walked by the sea shore and came to the ruins
of the great Abbey of Timoleague. With a heavy heart I
made this sad lament:

> O, empty roofless ruin
> Dwelling house and tower,
> Many stormy winds
> Have beaten on your walls,
> Much rain and cold
> And sea-gales you withstood
> Since you were offered first
> As shelter for Our Lord.
>
> Jagged walls mossed with grass
> Once a glory to this country,
> I grieve for your fall
> And your holy men sent wandering,
> Here now is loneliness
> No harmony within
> The harsh screech of the owl
> In place of chanted hymns.
>
> Ivy creeps on your arches
> Red nettles matt the floor
> The rangy fox whines thinly
> In crannies mumble stoats,
> Where the skylark sang out early
> To friars chanting hours,
> No clear sound now of tongues,
> But the jabbering of daws.
>
> No meat in your dining rooms
> No sun-bleached beds aloft,
> All that whiten in your shelter now
> Are honeycombs of bones,

Your nuns and Franciscans
Left you in great sorrow,
Your glebe without ceremony
Or a mass being said to God.

Attack and foreign cruelty
Base tyranny and malice
Strong arms and gross looting
Left you lonely as you are;

I, too, prospered once
But my character declined,
The world came against me
I am vigorless and blind,
My face is a twisted mask,
My heart a fruitless husk,
My friends lie in this graveyard
To turn reluctant dust—

If Death comes
I'll welcome him.

Seán Ó Coileáin

17
Goodbye to the Maigue

From *Filidhe Na Máighe* (The Maigue Poets), ed. An tAthair Pádraig Ua Duinnín (Dublin, 1906), p. 44.

In the Note to "Small Beer" (6), there is a description of Aindrias Mac Craith, the author of this poem, in his feud with Seán Ó Tuama. Mac Craith was "a roving, rambling schoolmaster" whose adventures with wine and women finally incurred the wrath of the local clergy and he was banished from his native region.

Goodbye to the Maigue

Goodbye to the Maigue
With its branches and berries,
Its hayricks and meadowlands,
Craftsmen and affluence,
Its stories and poems
And men of good will.

> O, I am laid low,
> Without friend or substance.

[71]

Without child or justice,
Without joy or love—
Turned out to loneliness.

Goodbye for ever
To the affable gentry
To the poets and clerics,
The learned conventions,
To friends free of bigotry,
Prejudice, cheating,
Flattery, anger, ill-will, deceiving.

Goodbye above all
To him who is bound
To my honey-sweet love
Who was kindly,
For her I am routed
To the moors for a spell,
No matter who she is—
I still love her.

Here I am wandering
Perished with cold,
Weakened, bent under sorrow,
Out on the mountain
With none on my side but
The freezing North wind and heather.

Alas, I am destitute,
Without sod or shelter,
From drinking and loving
I am left without vigor.

Aindrias Mac Craith

IV
Enemies

18
Evicted Woman

From *Cinnlae Amhlaoibh Ui Shúilleabháin* (The Diary of Humphrey O'Sullivan), ed. Michael McGrath S.J. (London, 1936), p. 21.

The poem is based on an episode described by Humphrey O'Sullivan in his Diary. On August 22, 1828, he was walking near his home in Kilkenny, a region where five families had been evicted from their cottages by Patrick Deveraux. O'Sullivan asked his way from a distraught woman who recounted her plight in the words of "Evicted Woman."

In his entry for September 25, the diarist reports that Deveraux's body has been found in a ditch, his head broken by an axe.

Evicted Woman

This is the road out of here
Through the potato field,
I planted them—but Deveraux will dig them—
Through the wheat field
My sons sowed it—but Deveraux will harvest it—
My Curse on him

Through the yard by my little wood pigeons,
They will roast in Deveraux's pot.

My own husband built this house,
I myself darkened the rafters with soot,
But Deveraux took the door off the jamb,
He took the hinges off the hooks
He left the house without a door,
The window without glass,
The hearth without a fire,
The sty without sow or sucking-pig,
Or boar, large or small, fat or lean.

I will never hear again
The anxious lowing of my cow to her calf
The whinny of my mare to her foal
The bleat of my sheep to her lamb
The call of my goat to her kid
The clucking of my hens to their chickens
The morning-call of my rooster.

I will not see again my white duck
Nor my speckled drake
Nor my honking goose
Nor my shining gander.

I will not see the bog-pool
Nor hear the cry of the bittern
Nor the shriek of the wild goose
Nor the small moan of the green plover
Nor the fluting of the moor plover
Nor the thin whine of the jack-snipe.

I will not see the crane
Nor hear the splashing of the water hen,
I will not dredge the pool
For the eel or the pike.
Far from here I will die
And my unhappy husband and my sad children

The sweet mint will not grow by my stream
Nor the red and white clover in my meadow,
I will not plant flax nor pull it
Nor steep it in the pond,
I will not turn my spinning wheel
I will twist no yarn.

My loom for wool and linen is thrown in the ditch
My chest is flung in the quarry
My table across the fence
My pans on the waste-ground
My chair out in the rain,
My pallet is without blanket or quilt,
My head has no covering
My back has no cloak.
> *For rent they are taken*
> *A hard cruel fate*

(from Amhlaoibh Ó Súilleabháin)

19
The Death of Dawson

From *Amhráin Sheáin Chláraigh Mhic Dhomhnaill* (The Poems of Seán Clárach Mac Domhnaill), ed. An tAthair Pádraig Ua Duinnín (Dublin, 1908), p. 51.

Seán Clárach Mac Domhnaill (1691–1754) was one of the famous group of Munster poets of the eighteenth century. He did not suffer the deprivations and miseries of most of the other poets of the time. But he was an ardent Jacobite supporter and on occasion had to go into hiding because of his political beliefs. He was chief poet of Munster and maintained the old tradition of holding periodical meetings of poets at his home.

The Penal Laws were in force during his lifetime and he saw his countrymen suffer under injustice and cruelty. One of the hated upholders of the system was Colonel James Dawson of Ballynacoorty in the Glen of Aherlow (formerly territory of the O'Briens). Dawson died in 1737 and Seán Clárach took the opportunity to write his famous *Aor* (Curse).

The Death of Dawson

Gravestones, guard your mouldy hoard in long keeping,
The bones of bloody treacherous whey-faced Dawson,
Famous not for gallantry in fights or wars
But for hanging, arson, robbery and beating.

Large was his expense in the sunlit mansion of O'Brien,
Fast locked his door and unwelcoming the halls,
In sheltered Aherlow where a gap divides the mountains
Harnessed to starvation his tenants toed the line.

His gates never opened at the pleas of feeble creatures,
No answer to their asking, no scraps fed their wasted frames,
If they took a few wood chippings, twigs or twisted branches
He flogged their bony haunches till the thin blood ran in
      streams.

May my curse overtake you without faltering or apology,
May Cocitus lap your grave in everlasting pain,
From Dublin to Cork may bloodhounds in full cry
Root in the rotten clay to worry your body.

This is Dawson's home now, stretched under these flags,
Who made vagabonds of farmers and destroyed many more,
Lonely women with small children walking the roads;
Forever may a turning spit roast you over flames.

His ways were set against the world and its laws,
A voracious immovable and bare-faced mongrel,
Forever tearing down the churches of God
May heaven for ever be shut to James Dawson.

Although great wealth was his for a while in this life
Heavy his judgment on the leaderless poor,
As drastic be the state prepared below in payment
Freezing cold and fierce thirst and raging heat assail you.

[79]

I am ravaged with sorrow that all your sort weren't choked
And John your useless son along with the rest of you,
As payment for every rampage you perpetrated
May a gang of mangy dogs with gusto macerate you.

May tight fetters bite and bind the legs of this monster
With sharp willow ropes from his home in Aherlow,
And string the villain up dangling among demons,
Damned be your soul forever, wolf, with this Decree.

Tombstones, press and bruise his jaw and filthy neck,
His eyes, his swollen tongue and black backside,
Heavy on every vein and joint of this creeping wreck,
In the hope that he and his like may never rise.

Seán Clárach Mac Domhnaill

20
Valentine Brown

From *Dánta Aogáin Uí Rathaille* (The Poems of Egan O'Rahilly), ed. Rev. Patrick S. Dinneen and Tadhg O'Donoghue (London, 1911), p. 30.

Aogán Ó Rathaille (1670–1726?) lived out his life in his native districts of Kerry and Cork. He is the greatest of the poets of the time and in his work is preserved the classical Irish mode in its purest form. Very little is known of his life, except that it was as miserable as most of his contemporaries'. He was very conscious of the tradition whereby the nobility were patrons and supporters of the poets. But during his lifetime the new families who replaced the Irish aristocracy did not have the appreciation of learning nor did they deem it their duty to support the wandering poets. Valentine Brown was Lord Kenmare, and he held estates that belonged formerly to the MacCarthys. There was no doubt in Aogán's mind that Brown had duties toward him as patron, just as he himself had duties as the patron's poet. He wrote a beautiful epithalamium on the marriage of Valentine Brown to Honoria Butler of Kilcash. However, when he applied for help when he was old, poor, and ill, he was rejected. He then wrote "Valentine Brown."

[81]

Valentine Brown

Darkness spreading over my age-crusted heart
As the foreign devils march through the green fields of Conn,
A cloud on the western sun whose right was Munster's throne,
—The reason I turn to you, Valentine Brown.

Cashel without company or horses, overgrown,
Brian's palace swamped with a black flood of otters,
No royal son of Munster ruling his own acres,
—The reason I turn to you, Valentine Brown.

The deer discarding the graceful shape by which she's known
Since the alien crow nested in the thick woods of Ross,
Fish leaving sunlit pools and hidden silent streams,
—The reason I turn to you, Valentine Brown.

Dar-Inish in the west mourning her earl of high renown,
In Hamburg, alas, our exiled noble lord,
An old gray eye weeping hard for all that is gone
—The reason I turn to you, Valentine Brown.

Aogán Ó Rathaille

V
Wanderings

21
A Halloween Chant— The Midnight Flitting of the Corpse and Tomás MacGahan

From Céad de Cheoltaibh Uladh (One Hundred Ulster Songs), ed. Enrí Ó Muirgheasa (Dublin, 1915), p. 46.

This is a folk story told in verse form. Douglas Hyde wrote down the same ballad and story, which he heard from an old man in Leitrim. He says "It is on Halloween night that one is especially liable to adventures like those of Tomaus O'Cahan, but it is well known that all gamblers coming home at night are exposed to such perils."

A Halloween Chant — The Midnight Flitting of the Corpse and Tomás MacGahan

"My walking through the night, MacGlynn,
Was a cause of mirth, of spiteful mirth,

With the damned corpse with no chance of burial
Amongst the deadmen, amongst the dead."

"Raise up my body without rejoicing
    And I'll give you a bullock, a fattened cow"
"If I agree to make this bargain
Where is the bullock, the fattened cow?"

"Small John Bingham, tall John Bingham,
They are my surety, they are my pledge,
I wrote an agreement in twisted scripture
To Bealan Assan, to Bealan Assan,

You will find a pot in the heap of lime,
Gray and ashy, ashy and gray,
Bring it with you under your arm
For food on the journey, food on the way."

The corpse was taken on Tomás's back
along the byeways, along the byeways,
by narrowing lanes, stony and gloomy
by the pale moonlight, by the pale moonlight.

A lengthy journey, sadly, crossways,
through drenching bogs, drenching moors,
west to Louth, great and holy,
of the grassy tombs, the grass-grown tombs.

"You will find a spade at your right hand
Behind the door, at the back of the door,
Strike a strong cut, a cut not faltering
Into the ground, down in the ground."

"I struck a strong cut, bold and deep
Into the ground, down in the ground,
Till I broke the shinbone of a foreign clown
Who was asleep there, who was asleep."

[86]

"Blast your guts" said the foreign trooper
"Where's my gun, is my pistol there?"
Said Mary Reilly, wife of Lord Guido
"Clear out of here, clear out of here."

> "Oro, Tomás, oh, oh, oh,
> Do not leave me, don't leave me here,
> There's the son of my mother's cousin in Creggan,
> Where I should be buried, I should be buried."

> *The corpse was taken on Tomás's back*
> *on its lonely tour, its lonely tour*
> *by roads that were narrow, stony and twisted*
> *by the light of the moon, light of the moon.*

"Sad, unhappy, I hurried down
On to Creggan, to Creggan More,
I found a spade at my right hand
Behind the door, behind the door.

Then I broke the jawbone of Watson Harford
Who was in the ground, down in the ground."
"Hububoo!" the blacksmith stammered
"Where's my hammer, where's my hammer?"

> "Oro, Tomás, oh, oh, oh,
> Don't leave me here, don't leave me here,
> Since I have an uncle's son in Derry
> There I'll be buried, there I'll be buried."

> *The corpse was taken on Tomás's back*
> *just as before, just as before,*
> *going weakly, worn-out, weary*
> *down to Derry, down to Derry.*

"When I got to the place I was bedraggled
With no courage left, no courage left,

The gates were strongly locked against me
And I pushed them hard, I pushed them hard."

"Defend your walls" Sir Walker calls,
"Or they'll be taken or they'll be taken,
Who knocks so hard? Each to his part
Come dead awaken, come dead awaken!"

> *Bones and coffins rose up straight*
> *out of the clay, out of the clay,*
> *and sat with no gap in an awful rage*
> *on top of the walls, on top of the walls,*

"A hundred damned curses" chorused the crowd
"What's the matter, what's the matter?"
"It's one of yourselves that's recently dead
Seeking burial, seeking burial,

"His cousin is here and that's the reason
Here you have him, here you have him."
"Who of his people is buried here
To claim admittance, to claim admittance?"

"I don't know the name or tribe of the madman
At the end of his life, the end of his life,
There's a shake and complaint left in him yet
So ask himself, ask himself."

22
The Adventures of
a Miserable Wretch

From *Eachtra Ghiolla an Amaráin* (The Adventures of a Luckless Fellow) by Donncha Rua Mac Conmara, ed. Tomás O Flannghaile (Dublin, 1897).

Donncha Rua was born in Cratloe, County Clare, about 1715 and died near Kilmacthomas in 1810. He wrote this poem around 1745, and it is traditionally believed to be a fanciful account of his own adventures on a trip to New-foundland.
(The underscored words and phrases occur in English in the original Irish version.)

The Adventures of a Miserable Wretch

Part One

I could tell famous stories to my friends
And turn high-flown words into verses nightly

About Brian Boru and that Fenian crowd
But I'd rather tell you what happened to me lately.

Along with most I was hungry and broke,
Flattened with cheating, injustice and lies,
Making do with bad checks in place of hard cash—
I was a school teacher in those days;
Everyone knows it's a bad occupation,
Scarcely a shilling I could get my hands on,
But thanks to the kindness of better-off neighbors
I divided my evenings between women and brandy.

One night I was lying alone in bed
Thinking awhile of the state of the country,
Of my life being spent without clothes or gold—
I'd as well be shoveling dirt or wed.

Should I leave for ever my Irish home
Where once I was nearly a priest ordained
And sail with a tail wind far away,
Perhaps as far as New England's shore?

      Next day I got up early
      Grasped my stick and set out lightly
      With my hat forthrightly tilted
      To find a ship that fairly slanted
      From the hills of holy Ireland.

Friends and neighbors came to see me off
Though some not sorry at my sudden going,
Those who begrudged a drink of buttermilk,
Mean Malachy who rarely parted with a farthing.

Oh, be it known to the Aristocracy and Powers
The quantities of victuals, drinks and wares
Bestowed upon me by my gathered kinsmen,
To nourish me in trouble, without shrinking:

[90]

First a huge oak chest I myself could fit in,
Within twelve dozen eggs of mottled birds,
A crock of butter and a slab of streaky bacon,
Nine stone of oats, a barrel of red potatoes.

I got a keg of ale that would improve with keeping
And put life in dead bones if they'd a kick left in them,
Long-sleeved plaid shirts and brocade waistcoats,

In the chest were my shoes, a wig and a beaver
And more of the like I won't now account for.

The first leg of my journey took me to Waterford
In the steps of that brave old hero Conán,
By a bit of good luck I got room and board
At the house of the prettiest girl in Ireland.

> She was curly-haired and clever,
> A practiced hand at drawing porter
> And knew all the local scandal
> But she'd throw you out in anger
> If you ran out of cash.
> Telling a secret's not my aim
> But my joking made her smile,
> She added to my fame
> And made it worth my while.

Soon she was powdering my wig till it gleamed
And bringing me brandy for the morning after,
My shirts were laundered and starched and ironed,
Her welcoming kindness had me quite bowled over.

> But her mother asked for payment;
> For every pint and sandwich
> She demanded an advance.

A few brief days I stayed at that inn,
Waiting for a ship to sail from Ireland;

I met Captain Allen, a light-hearted man,
And I quickly arranged to sail with him.

I packed my things and left my mistress,
My trunk and myself on the road together,
I got to Passage on a horse and cart
With a load of herrings providing ballast.

The port officials were drunkards and fools—
I spoke no English but could manage in Latin—
The clerk made an effort to get my name
And in the daybook he scratched "MacNamara."

My trunk was smoothly hoisted on deck,
I retired to the stateroom for a drink and a smoke,

The ship set sail at the high noon of Phoebus
And Aeolus and Thetis helped set her course.

They drove the ship in a nor'west direction,
She scudded away from the heat of the sun,
Soon those sons of Magnus were sorely affected
By the endless sky and the heaving ocean.

An untouched meal sat in front of Teddy O'Leary,
Not a bit nor drop could his stomach keep down,
Kilty O'Keefe was crying for his wife
But his tears were bringing him no relief;
Peter O'Dowd crouched in a corner
Puking all over Phelim's cloak,
Gerry collapsed along with Flann and
Carl and Conn in a drunken bout.
Carbry and Garrett and Toby looked promising
Tapping my ale-keg to stave off the vomiting;
Sean O'Trahy retched in the scuppers,
Groaning at every gripe in his stomach,
Dermot voiced the common opinion—
The half of us would never return to Ireland.

[92]

Thus in suffering they passed the days,
Broken, exhausted, prostrate, shrunken,
I, too, like a corpse afflicted with death
Lay stretched on the deck as wretched as one of them.

I'm ashamed to speak of my degradation—
Not long since I was the King of the Wits,
Now the butt of the crowd and the fool of the fair,
Beseeching God for a friendly storm
To steer us back to our former home.

Better for me than owning riches—
Even as much as Croesus—
Or the golden fleece
Stolen by the son of Aeson,
Or the power of the Scots and Dalriada,
Or the prize in a draw of Deirdre
Who ruined the sons of Usna,
Or the booty left by George in Flanders
When he scampered for refuge to Hanover—
To be at home in a safe harbor
Recovering my health in the friendly Barony,
Chanting my verses and teaching my class,
Listening to the priest while he filled my glass,
Or chatting with Peter Kennedy in Kill
Or in Georgetown with Richard Bawn
(He is a gentleman and a Power)
Or with my own cousins in Cratloe,
The Cullen clan, it's hard to beat them,
Or in beery Limerick on the Shannon
Where I often drank my fill of pints,

Or in Slieve Gua that took first place
In welcoming students, singers and poets,
Where the greatest of all, the learned O'Moran,
Would make me a proper ancient ode for my deathbed.

Or a hundred other good things that have slipped my
  mind—
A common lapse for one who is tired.

Part Two

Listen a while, I'll continue the story:
After our agony—every word is the truth—
Into my dreams while my mind was still weakened
Came the fairywoman, quiet and good.

Her hair fell straight and loose to the ground,
Her cheek was curved and smooth as a rowanberry,
Her beauty led me truly to believe her
Eevul, the devious witch of Carrig-lee.

She took me to the mouth of a cave full of wind,
In a barren place with gray bushes and heather,
I asked the pale and ghostly woman
To what strange wandering I was committed.

She said "Hold my hand tightly till we return
And you will never be in danger,
I will show you for your wonder
Sights not seen by men of Thomond."

Down we drift, our hands firmly clasped,
Down in the dim cave with the daylight fading,
Before us the shores of the bitter channel,
Beside us the flowing of frigid Acheron.

Those who have died follow the same road,
Each soul and ghost held forfeit for payment,
Thousands were waiting with tearful faces
Seeing they had arrived there without the fare.

[94]

It was not lack of burial as in the Aeneid,
But this crowd had wasted their wages on drink,
Now they lacked a token to pay the ferry
Unless they could scrounge a ha'penny by begging.

I've heard from those who read and hold forth
That the ferryman there is leathery Charon,
But they're liars all I can easily prove,
It was the famous strongman of Irish stock
Old Fenian Conán, that gallant pilgrim,
We saw in the boat, rowing it diligently.

The skin of a black sheep covered his backside
But there were other signs by which we knew him,
He charged a sixpenny toll to all the English,
And Latin and Gaelic were his only language.

When he saw myself and sweet Eevul there
He tossed his bald head with a dreadful glare
And like a bull let out a roar,
"You cursed clod, you hag, you whore!
How dare you bring one in human form
To where no scrap of earth came before,
It were worth my while to exert my power
And flay you both till you're sick and sore!"

"Easy, my hero," said the gentle lady,
"Leave off your fury and be a bit more cool,
A man in affliction I found in a swoon,
A descendant of Ireland's ancestral leaders."
Then Conán grasped and squeezed my fingers
And gave a loud laugh, a glorious shout,
At the noise of his voice the heavens trembled,
The whole crowd heard it and the pit of Hell shook.

We cross the stream in the narrow black boat
And take a short cut to a haunted hill,

[95]

We arrive in front of an unlocked gate,
A place where a mad dog howled at will.
No lie did Virgil set down in his verses—
This was the persecutor of peacemakers, Cerberus.

The mad dog was asleep in the middle of the track,
Wisps of hay under him, wheezing and snoring.
Then that greatest champion of Irish seed
Grabbed him viciously and throttled his throat,
He never let the hound give a turn or twist
Till we bounded across him, scared out of our wits.

We continued our way to the top of the mound
And stopped, and thought, and looked around.

Troops were rushing about on all sides,
Dragging and grabbing and tearing and chasing;
Conán said he'd give us an explanation,
An account of those armies and their battle frenzy:
"See there beyond the great sons of Gadelus
And the flock of spirited girls of Ireland,
Watch how they gouge out that other gang galloping,
Tearing up roots to maim them and blind them.

"The Fenius Fearsa are kicking out and routing
The defeated Danaans, scattering and slicing them,
Do you see there Donn with his razor-edged sword
Flinging off heads to where feet ought to be!
Do you see those sturdy men of Greece and Troy,
Hector with his sword declaiming his heroism,
Gray-haired Anchises enfeebled with age,
And the laboring there of Romulus and Remus
Building stone-strength to buttress their reign!
Do you hear the murmuring of the horde of poets,
Singing their songs, gaming and sporting,
Horace inveigling his beloved Maecenas
And unceasingly scalding the rest with his satire,

Ovid on a bench there writing to Caesar,
And Juvenal with his pen dripping gall and bile,

"And golden-haired Hugh MacCurtin from Ireland,
His verses sweet-voiced in melodious Gaelic,
An insinuating prince of poets enticing them,
The sound of his voice beguiling even the dying!

"Do you see that gloomy group of men kept apart?
Like giants their heads tower over the Cyclops;
They are, alas, a troop of the Fenians,
Supple and vigorous, high-strung and nervous.

"Ah, Finn MacCool, famous for death-dealing blows,
If you and I could return to our downtrodden land
We would ease and comfort the poor with companion-
          ship
And give assistance and refuge to the learned sages,
We would bring home again the soldier-son of James
And get help too from Scotland, if I had a say in it.

"Take a good look at Luther who altered religion
And at thick-skinned Calvin sweating off the lard,
At Henry the Eighth and beside him his queen,
All swinging by chains from gibbets harsh.

"Every Englishman passing has to give them a wallop.
That tricky quartet who perverted our priests,
But those who are free you see without fetters
Will go with the son of God to live in peace.

"Now home you go" said our valiant host,
"As Irish ambassador say this from us:

"Not long will our people and James the Pretender
Be ground down by a king who hates our guts,
A leader will rise of the seed of Aiver

Who will cure injustice and throw out the invader,
The crown will be his reward for endeavor
And the Milesian breed will live forever.

"Avoid the evil that destroyed Eve's children,
Take up prayer and penance and the Crown of Thorns,
Be kind and giving and love your neighbor
And maybe you'll make it to heaven yet.

"I must get on, they're shouting and calling,
That bunch of Lutherans has my stomach in knots.
The French have killed and despatched a thousand,
And now I must haul them all across!"

With that he sprang from my sight with a leap,
And cleverly Eevul took me off speedily,
We came back in a manner not too clear to me
Driven like a rabbit from a hole with a stick.

At once I was awake from my cloudy dream,
My own bed under me, my trunk there and my clothes:
It was thus I discovered my fever had abated,
And the ship was drawing ahead at full speed.

But my heart was sad at the recollection
That all I'd seen was hallucination.

The man in the crow's-nest up near the main-top
Saw in the distance a ship bearing down,
"Helm-a-lee!"—I was glad for some action—
Roared Captain Allen in anger and passion
"Gunner, give fire! we'll fight the naygurs,
We'll conquer or die, my Irish hayroes!"
"All hands aloft!"—I dashed out in my shirt
With a sharp-edged cutlass grasped in my fist,
A gun and a pistol tucked in their places;

[98]

Thunderous roaring and flashing around us,
The ships alongside, we hacked at the ropes—
Emptying our guns in each others' decks.
Madness and fury and violent clashing,
Uproar and raging and strife and blazing,
Yelling and crashing and weeping and screaming!

They heard it in Cork, though a long way away,
The frightful din of the battle that day.

It was a lively French frigate, rangy and lean,
That put us in that fix and filled us with fear,
Under the fire of forty guns in array,
As soon as we could we decided to flee
Staking our fate on a fast getaway.

Our blood lay lapping in lakes on the maindeck,
Under my breast in my side I'd a wound,
At the end of the fight I was stabbed in the back,
Severed bodies and heads sprawled scattered around.

"Haul yards, stand by, and hoist the mainsail!
Haul tacks and sheets and free the stay-sails!"

In the end we were taken, it's only the bare truth,
And penned in the hold all together in pain,
Without a taste of food since the morning before,
Fainting and moaning and next to death's door.

But we didn't lie long without devising a plan,
We needed some strength to attempt an escape,
We spotted the barrel of beer beside us,
We drank it in gulps till we emptied the keg.

Then we smashed through the hatch and emerged in the
    stern—

[99]

Louis' rabble took fright like a shepherdless flock,
Fifty Frenchmen were soon overcome in our power
And we locked them below in the hold in their turn.

We faced to the east at the sinking of Phoebus
On an even set course in the direction of Ireland.
Twenty French died in that unlucky engagement—
I'm not counting the number who were injured severely.

We lost three of our crew in the morning early,
Amputations and wounds marred more than fifteen,
A bullet took the Captain's boy—no loss to me—
He once stole my cap and laughed at my shivering.

At last we reached Passage, battered and pallid;
I rode off to Waterford alone at a canter.
Almost a month, worn-out and grieving
I lay in my bed until God's Son cured me.

I went home quickly, it was a relief to me.
It is truly no mockery, no lie, nor a boast,
Never again will I set foot on a boat,
Barring I'm dragged there tied down with ropes!

A fitting end: Thanks be to Christ for all things,
Protect me, Friend, do not betray us, King of Kings,
Oh Lord of Heaven who bought us dearly
From the fetters of wordly sin relieve us,
Withhold your anger, give us strength to live,
Save our souls—there you have my story!

The Adventures of a Miserable Wretch

To This Point

Donncha Rua Mac Conmara

[100]